RELEASE
THE HOUNDS

Misty Cosgrove

NeoPoiesisPress.com

ℛ

NeoPoiesis Press, LLC

2775 Harbor Ave SW, Suite D, Seattle, WA 98126-2138
Inquiries: Info@NeoPoiesisPress.com
NeoPoiesisPress.com

Release the Hounds
ISBN 978-0-9892018-8-9 (pbk)

1. Poetry. I. Cosgrove, Misty.

Library of Congress Control Number: 2015910751

First Edition

Cover Design: Milo Duffin and Stephen Roxborough

Printed in the United States of America.

Dedicated to... My Huckleberry

Contents

Bruised Muscadines

Her eyes were cold blue saucers
chipped around the edges
from late night beatings
under a pink calico quilt
from a man
that knew to stay
just above the knee
where soft yellow ruffles
outlined the hem
of her Sunday school dress.

His long anxious fingers
pierced the rusted wire
that ran behind
a Muscadine tree
when Mama scrubbed away
the pale red proof
in the washtub.

Floyd's Barber Shop

I pitched enough fits
to win a seat in the Buick
and go along for the ride
into town.

I waited inside a dual exhaust steel cage
while my brother and Daddy
rubbed elbows with the elite members
of the (We have a penis and you don't) club.

Killing time consisted of sniffing
empty packs of smokes
while holding a Phillips Head screwdriver
between my legs and imagining my conversation
with Floyd.

"Afternoon Floyd,
I'm just needing a trim."

"Sorry baby girl,
you have to have a penis
to be in here with us."

"What the Hell do you call this?"
*shaking the Phillips Head up and down
Between my legs.*

"Oh, my apologies. Please, come sit
in chair number three, right between your
father and brother. I'll have you fixed up
in no time."

Before I could imagine my new haircut
my Daddy opened the car door
and hollered at me to hop in the back
and let my brother ride up front.

Green Tomatoes

The heat follows me
while I walk through his garden
my basket is empty.

I can't find the courage
to take my pick.
Henry said to take what I wanted
but not the tomatoes, they're
not ripe.
I want the fat green one
hanging midway
down the wire cage.
I could snag it
fill my basket with pole beans
and hide my shiny prize.
The plump emerald
could be my little secret.

Henry's got secrets.
All ex-soldiers do.
Henry might punish me
if he finds it.

Beneath a shady patch of vines,
carve his initials
on my forehead.
A knife slicing through
young, taut skin,
like that of an enemy.

Pierre

The nubile Bluefins
fought over the mouthbrooder
every season.

He performed his dance
in the murky river
along the waterlogged bank.

Pierre could wrangle
the toughest of nightcrawlers
from death's looped tongue.

The wide eyed felines
swooned in unison
as Pierre flexed
his phosphorescent side armor
and flared his swollen whiskers.

One by one
he embraced the enamored females
and planted his seed.

Pierre was a gentleman.
When it was time to harvest,
he tucked his spawn
into the warm riverbed below,
hovered patiently over his young
while the females escaped downstream.

They all swam at hypersonic speeds,
weaving in and out of streams
hoping that the guilt
would never catch up.

Cussing Out a Chicken After You Throw Crackers in His Face

Black beady eyes,
boiling acid in a nervous gut
with a scraggly truckstop mouth
stinging like an old leather belt
across the back of my thighs.

"Quit staring at me
with that look of entitlement
you dirty fucking chicken.
I'm the only one who showed up
to feed your rotten ass
and I don't appreciate being pecked at
through the wires.
Yeah he's dead
and I'm not sure what the future
holds for you,
but I'm here now
with a pack of crackers.
Stop trying to figure shit out
and fill your belly while you can."

Hooves

The Hospital's on call Pastor
barged in the room
trying to hold my hand.

I kindly asked him to leave.

He begged me to allow
his little song and dance.

"You got two minutes." I said

He quickly shuffled his hooves
over to your bedside,
salivated over your body
like a child molester
hiding beneath a slide
on the playground.

"Are you almost done?" I asked.
"One more verse my child."

I dreamed of ripping the tubes
out of your throat
and wrapping them around his neck,
holding tight
until his voice grew
as silent as yours.

Trash Bags

Talking to this cheap
military issue headstone
is getting me nowhere.
I need to see his face.
Dig his rotten ass up
and share a cigarette.

Nobody would notice.

None of the grieving
have time to visit.
Busy spending their death check
on new fake nails
and leather boots.
I should just dig him up
and throw him in my trunk.

I might need some trash bags,
he's been in there a while.
He could make a guest appearance
on Thanksgiving.
His heartbroken wife would love it.
She could introduce her dead husband
to the man she was fucking
the day he died.

"Take care of your Mama." He said.

"No need to, the man who stole your toolbox
has it under control. But don't worry, he looks
like a jackass wearing your Waylon Jennings shirt."

Hutch is Thinking About Nam

The Buick backfires
and he jumps
to the floorboard.

He knocks your bowl of rice
off the table
screaming about
Gook babies
floating in the fields.
Mama interjects,

"Go eat that shit in your room baby."

He gives the first piece of pizza
that the stoned Asian guy delivers
to the dog.
Makes you watch the dog
for twenty minutes
to see if he's been poisoned.

While you're sitting on the toilet,
you notice him
behind the shower curtain.
He's sitting in the tub
eating a can of beanie weenies.

"Beanie weenies worked like currency
in the Bush."

Signs your birthday card:

Take no Prisoners.
Kill the Wounded.
Eat the dead.

Stranger

It wasn't the kind remark you made
that trapped me in this tank.
The hostile exchange
was the hook
I swallowed.
Words became evidence
of a moment
that was being noticed.
My thoughts were swimming
in your mind too.
Throwing away my words
no longer brought sadness,
knowing that you brought them
in from the cold
and kept them safe and warm.
I awake in the hopes
that you'll appear
above my tank,
but only dead fish
look down at me
through the salty water.
They stare at my tentacles,
trying to connect,
create suction
against the glass.
They don't know about my two hearts.
We just share glances,
while I wait for you.

Guilt

Walter's wife confronts me
while I'm bartending.
She's watched her husband
sink for years,
slowly being strangled
by a disease.
A disease that I profit from.

"Please don't serve Walter anymore.
He needs help. He's starting re-hab.
I'm trying to save my family."

I am a vulture.
The black-winged scavenger
picking rotten flesh
off the ruined.
A drug dealer
stealing story time from little girls
who need their Daddy
tucking them in at night,
instead of drunk on a barstool.

The world is full of vultures.
The cashier at the liquor store
was a vulture too.
She used to give me a lollipop
when Daddy bought his whiskey
on Friday.
I hated her for poisoning him,
but I always took the candy.

Sweethearts

We are a rare breed.

You with your graceful cunning
and stealth like accuracy
for ripping out the hearts
of the doe eyed.

Me with my crass strength
and insatiable hunger
to lick your wounds.

Two proud beasts
destroying the magic
that binds them.

Molasses

I am a black fingered witch
consuming more
than her fair share
cast out by the virtuous.

My accuser covets my appetite
but has never even opened up
a menu.

Suck in Your Gut

Mama grew five babies in her rotten womb.
She branded them on their forehead with the cherry
of a cigarette as soon as they shot out of her
Vagina.
This birthmark would later serve to help
the five find each other, after they ran
away in the dark.

The five lost touch after Bruce handcuffed
Mama. Bruce was the police officer that Mam
accused of having a little squirrel dick.

"What you gonna do about it, you little
squirrel-dick-having motherfucker?"

Soft Cock

The pasty fleshed starfish
is suspended in acrobatic display.
His moist skin coated with a fine sheen
of chlorine beads.

The sun is an oven.
Wake up and shine,
round buttery tip,
and glisten like
the golden skin of a biscuit.

I Paid Someone to Kill My Dog

Aside from the hair shedding,
the new dog is alright.
I thought about giving him
the hollowed out tennis ball
with a treat inside.
The previous owner won't mind.
I haven't seen him in over three years.
The vet taped a garbage bag
around his waist
to keep her floors clean.
Killing a dog makes their bowels release.
I had him cremated.
I wonder about the guy that burns dogs
all day for a living.
Does he try not to look at their face
before he puts them in the oven?
Does he think about killing his wife?
Getting to work early
and throwing her in with the dogs…

Lucy

She slices her way through the sticky fog,
steamy waters of the swamp
guide her thick frame
down the bulk of the river.

She stops to frolic in a bed of lilies
when the call of an unknown male
brings the jaunty rhythm of her day
to a screeching halt.

The bellow of her suitor is so strong
that she longs for instant repetition.
She traces the sound of his cry
to a soggy nest of branches
collected around the trunk
of a dewy skinned Cypress.
Jim's voice continues to grow
louder and louder, while beads of water
dance ferociously
off his reverberating back.

She will spend the morning with Jim.
The soft bed of lilies will still be there
when she returns.

Mrs. Wilson

The invitation I received can only mean one thing,
you're not dead yet.

I'll arrive just in time to watch you salivate
while the new grandbaby gets passed around
the crowd of jackals.

I'll stare at your leather curled toes
while you force a smile at me
for the sake of the creepers.
They like to sniff your fat clammy fingers
while you sleep, hoping for some sign
that death has begun to feed.

Ugly Duckling

She came walking up the street
as I was backing down the driveway.
Teenaged and husky
with no visible female attributes
detectable in the dark corner
of my rear view mirror.
Unsure of twenty year old drum brakes,
I yell at the figure,

"Hey man, you might want to back up
For just a minute."

Budding breasts hidden under an oversized t-shirt
were the first clue.
Next was the plump, troubled face
sucking on a stolen cigarette.
She looked at the ground as I drove by.
I turned up the radio in an attempt
to push the guilt out the windows.
I wanted to drive back by
and say something that would let her know
I see her.
Young lady, Miss, girl, anything to take away
the extra weight I had put on her shoulders.

Special Needs Hank

"The trick to getting a grub out is Vaseline.
Smear a bit on top of the wound and wait
five minutes. The jelly smothers him and
prevents any oxygen from getting in.
Wipe the Vaseline off and his little head
will come peeking out of the dog's flesh.
That's when you snatch him with the tweezers
and hope he comes out in one piece. Then just
burn the body with a lighter."

"That is disgusting, and I'm sorry I asked."

My neighbor doesn't like Special Needs Hank.
He can't appreciate a bald coonhound that
keeps running into an electric fence.
Hank forgets once a month and goes
to sniff the wire.
The juice runs through his wet nose
and off he goes.

Yelping and Running in Circles

The grubs are all gone and the mange
is clearing up, but his mind isn't firing
on all eight cylinders. It never was.
At first glance, I thought Hank was
just a bony bag of purple skin, sitting
inside a box outside the grocery store.
Black dead eyes peeking out from
diseased flesh.
Rotten thing might be better off dead I thought,
until he howled. The most intense rumble that
I felt in my gut. All the energy in his body
came through in his call. I was instantly smitten
with the sound and wanted to hear it again,
even if it meant a problem dog.
Hank will chew it of it's on the floor.
He shit out a purple crayon with the
label still on it.
He's scared of bees, lawnmowers,
and my cell phone ring.
If I yell at him, he pisses himself.
But at night, he howls.

High and Mighty

The warm welcome you received
says nothing about the role you play.
I would show the same amount of courtesy
to a stray dog.
Hiding behind the Devil doesn't make you
untouchable.
That no count bastard walks the line
because I tell him to.
The next time you hold his hand
under my table,
I'll chop it off at the wrist
and I promise you
he won't even raise an eyebrow.

Fancy Christmas Card

It casts a shadow over the competition
atop my mantle.
Glossy stock paper
and professionally taken photos,
make her card the pinnacle
of sent wishes.
I'm just not sure the collage
captures the real essence
of family life.
I can't recall her fondness for sitting
under an oak tree
on a vintage quilt
with her husband and kids
all wearing matching shirts.
I don't remember the festive gathering
where they drank hot cocoa
next to a grand piano,
each hand cupping a shiny red mug
filled to the brim with marshmallows
that never seem to melt.

"I was expecting a picture of her husband
on the computer at three in the morning
jacking off to Asian Porn.
She hasn't touched his dick
in over eight months
and dreams about him being killed
so she can be a widow."

I keep this thought to myself,
and slide my fingers across
the raised gold lettering of
"Happy Holidays"

Kennesaw Mountain Battlefield

She's riding alone in the seat
of a half sucked
lemonhead yellow school bus.

She gently places moist hands
under skinny denim clad legs
and floats on the warm sweat
that refuses to absorb
into the slick green vinyl bench.

Men died here,
and the leaves smell like mildew
from a Confederate flag
that fell behind a washing machine.

Parent Teacher Conference

Shrivelled soul of a dictator
that reigns over tiny limbs
molding their young minds
into a platoon of soldiers.

The child army will take their rightful place
in the lead one day
and wash your flesh and blood
down their gullets
with a carton of chocolate milk.

Sportsbar Whore

I knew a woman with bad skin
and a sense of fairness.
She serviced men out back
behind the trash can.

"I don't charge the Mexicans
any more than the white dudes."

My co-workers despised her and
didn't want her using the same
bathroom as them.
But I couldn't tell her apart
from the wait staff.
They both pushed their breasts up
and reapplied their lipstick every hour,

I took a cigarette break every hour.
I once asked the whore if she had a lighter
and she told me,
"I don't smoke, that's a nasty habit."

The Moon is Following

He changes shape
depending on my daily chores.

A freight train running through
a field of raspberries, he fills a basket
while I sit in traffic.

He's a giant Magnolia
puckering up to the sun,
allowing the wind to blow his scent
across my front porch.

He's a thief breaking in my window.
His pale light lying next to me
on my bed, like a gentleman
waiting to dream.

Slaughterhouse

She liked to explain her philosophy on men
when we walked to the gas station.
Once there, she could convince
any minimum wager with a dick
to buy her a pack of Kent Golden Lights.
Men leaning and posing against a brick wall
while she seemed to dance around them.
Men that looked like bags of trash
ripped open and strewn across the parking lot.
She was a handful of glitter
sprinkling herself over the debris.

These men don't have faces.
Their blurry features prevent me from
branding them with a name.
Just big sacks of meat
being herded like cattle
to the slaughterhouse
between her legs.

Mama Loved Satan and Sweet Baby Jesus

Her devotion to the Devil was the only thing
she was ever faithful to.
She would drop sweet baby Jesus
down an abandoned well
if sin came along.
She just picked Baby Jesus back up
the next day
and asked for forgiveness.

Like most Southern Baptists,
Mama thought it necessary
to tell her children of the Devil's plan
to steal our thoughts.
She made me write down all the bad things
I could imagine
and burn the paper
in the backyard.
The ashes would float up to heaven
where Jesus would purify them.
I once told Mama that Satan was powerless.
The writer who created such a character
had the real power.

Scion

He remains the luminous star
that burns into the center of existence
pulling all life into its revolution.

You became a rain soaked matchstick
crumbling against the abrasive back
now turned on you.

Jealousy gnawed away
the last scrap of substance
that hung off your surly frame,
leaving me with a rotten corpse
to embrace behind closed doors.

Bingo Night at the VFW

Miss Betty's shrine sparkles
under the dim legion lights.
Polished and poised
David's medals glisten
behind a thin glass frame.
Chained to a memory
that she pins to her chest,
she nervously waits for a warm body
to acknowledge her efforts.

I watch from a distance
as her crisp yellow pantsuit
and matching hairbow
go unnoticed
in a sea of pastel sweatpants.

Youngins

The line to buy tickets is winding past the sidewalk.
The man behind me has no sleeves on his shirt.
His thick mound of armpit hair
has little deodorant snowflakes that sprinkle
when he scratches and grunts.

The kids in front of me are bubbling over
like a nervous milkshake.
They're holding hands and staring at the ground.
They smell like pencil shavings and scantron sheets.

They'll combine their money to buy popcorn
and a soda to share.
They have no idea what a sub-prime mortgage is.

Concrete Lambs

The sausage biscuit
I had for breakfast
began to battle for territory
with the red eye gravy
somewhere between
The French Impressionists
and Verrocchio's David.

I scurried along the ivory steps
passing immortalized beauties
who seemed to be taunting me
with their acrylic stares.

I saw the bathroom sign
just a few feet away
and began to walk
at a steady pace.
A sculpture of concrete lambs
stopped me dead in my tracks.
A heaping mess of Jesus
lay spilled out before me
with my drunk, dead Grandpaw
mixed in the mortar.

I sat silently at the altar
while Howard Finster hurled
cheap whiskey fueled sermons at me
through an old familiar voice.
Throwing me backwards in time
to a sun dried Alabama front porch,
a skeleton standing at the pulpit,
and a child who couldn't believe.

Old Man Williams

The Bingo hall intermission
is when he spreads the charm,
laying it thick like hot molasses
on a pan of yesterday's biscuits.
Turning embedded wrinkles
into giddy schoolgirl smiles.

A crisp, plaid button-up shirt
frames Willie's soft skeletal face,
while heavily starched brown slacks
shoot straight down into polished loafers.

He stops at the ladies table
and delivers a grin, a joke,
and enough attention from a man
to warm even the most neglected hearts.

He walks past the table of men
and their latest discussion of politics
with the greedy smirk of a young boy
who doesn't want to share his bag of cookies.

Sore Loser

He liked his women shy
and his pancakes thick and electric.
Maple covered lightning bolts
and giddy hesitation kept him
suckling at the titty.

Boldness in the destruction of property.

He'll cut the eyes out of your
Waylon Jennings album cover
and slide his tongue
through the Outlaw's mouth,
slap the exposed pink meat
with a hot spatula
and he'll leave pouting
without cleaning his plate.

Huckleberry

Their paycheck stubs are misleading.
In order for them to have it all,
they would need my spot on the porch swing
watching your middle toe stick out
half an inch past the others
and every sugar dusted pecan
that hides in the ice cream cone
we're sharing.

Bigot

His meaty face whiskers
marinating
in twelve year old scotch,
hearty rich man chuckles
expose a curtain
of dry neglected dentures
when Big Papa Bear
shows off
his thick brown baby
to the envious onlookers.
Plump tongue moistens the tip,
sticky fingers twirl the girth
and haggard lips clutch tightly
to form a most intimate suction.
So he needs a moist Presidente
throbbing inside his mouth
when he makes fun of gay men.
I'm sure it's nothing.

Rise of the Fuzzy Ones

There was a rumble brewing
deep in the bellies of all deck dwellers.
I had ignored the warnings
of my own clan members,
"You gotta kill them big ass bees girl,
they gonna make holes in your porch."
It wasn't that easy I explained.
I had respect for the carpenter clan.
They protected me from the Wasp predators
who long to rule over the back yard territory.
Me and the fuzzy ones had established
a peaceful solution for cohabitation
when I first built the deck.

But my alcoholic neighbour,
wearing a Tasmanian Devil t-shirt, was right.
The fuzzy ones were building an army
of epic proportions with every new hole.
Hundreds of brood lay inside,
each larvae filled opening
just waiting for their day of glory
when they can buzz around
and smack me upside the head
while I'm carrying a plate
of grilled hot dogs.
Those meat tubes
falling through the wooden railing
and thumping against the hood
of a broken down lawnmower
meant first blood had been drawn.

Hungover at the Birthday Party

When a princess turns nine,
she wants to be at the roller rink
with a plastic crown on her head,
skating in a circle with her friends,
dreaming with the music.
The loudest speakers in the world
are at the roller rink.
They pump out kiddie dance jams
that send euphoric pleasure
into the minds of little kids.
I look for their smiles.
Hard to see though from the wall
I'm clinging to.
I move to the inner circle
like an eighteen wheeler
backing up.
Slow movements and a pack of crackers
is the plan.
If I sit in the middle and eat my crackers,
maybe some of their energy
will form a protective circle around me
and keep me from puking
at this little girl's party.
She is a princess,
and I don't want to be that ugly old witch
throwing poison apples into the crowd.

Slobber Bone

Leave that chicken leg sitting on the table
and he'll snatch it up and run for the hills.
His sneaky streak is ready to take on
all your threats.
Damaged souls don't cower like the fortunate do.
They bare teeth and take the punch.
Hank hides his treasure of chicken legs,
leather boots, and dirty panties
in the house I built him.
He stays where it's safe now.

Quitting Smoking

Thirty degrees outside means he'll go in the basement to smoke. The
vents carry the smell into our room, infusing my pillow with a
reminder of something I miss dearly since quitting. Jealousy makes
my blanket scratchy,
The fan noisy, and his presence intolerable.

"Why can't you go on the porch to smoke?
The room smells like a fucking pool hall."

"Anything your highness wishes of course, next time
I'm on the porch."
Compliance irritates me and denies my need for pain.
If he lashed out at me, I could chase him away. Chasing him away
would give me an excuse to fail. Failure could be followed by a
cigarette, followed by a glass of wine,
Followed by familiar ground.

While I'm lying on my side thinking of new ways to sabotage, his
wiry chest hair warms my back, arms squeeze around my frame, and
his soft penis finds a cubby to rest in between my thighs.

Chain Break

A rich history of violence
sits deep below the surface
of lollipop smeared kisses
and tadpole adventures.

An arsenal of biological weapons
lay dormant in the blue eyed boy
with the brim-full smile.

Shining and skipping
past the sun,
he consumed the hours
of a Sunday afternoon
while fate stood caged
inside the empty howls
of a forgotten purebred.

Mama's Outbursts

The smart moms with big teeth,
big, bright, picket fence teeth,
all say the same things.
No television and no junk food.
I ponder this while me and my son
are eating Pop-Tarts and watching cartoons.
I should make him go read a book,
but I'm selfish.
Being an adult is a game.
I fouled early on thanks to a childhood
in the nose bleed seats.
I couldn't see the plays through
drunk painted faces.
The mom from *Little House on the Prairie*
was my dream.
She smelled like peppermint
and wanted to show me the fine art of butter churning.
She never stabbed a man
or made perverted comments
about Tom Selleck's moustache.

"I'll bet he's got some whiskers
in them pants too."

I wanted to tell that dirty bitch to shut up
and forbid the showing of Magnum P.I.
My Dad refused to stifle her outbursts.
He found them amusing.

Old Enough to Bleed, Old Enough to Breed

Is the mantra they live by.

They wear tight blue jeans,
chain wallets, and leather work boots
that cost more than their wedding ring.
They grab their dicks in line
while holding a sausage biscuit
and a cup of coffee.
Multi-tasking the way their wife did
while she was raising all their babies,
and they brag,

"Hell naw, I didn't change no diapers."
Time has passed,
and the babies stand next to their father in line.
They watch him grab his dick
and make thrusting motions with their hips
in the direction of a teenage girl.
The boy is learning first hand
how to be a man.

Their mother tells the ladies in church
how fast her boys are growing.
She used to be that fresh meat
not yet divided.
A young doe running through the woods.
A dusty old trophy now,
mounted on the couch rather than the wall.

Blubber

He swam up to me while I sat on the dock.
Slick vinyl skin and a handsome grin,
the whale who flicked his tail.

"I don't need Visine, I'm winking at you."

Once invited, I dive into his mouth,
make a comfy nook inside his belly,
sew window treatments to match his
baleen curtains.

My friends throw message bottles into the
sea, trying to warn me of danger.

"This whale can't be trusted. He wants to
drag you to the bottom of the ocean floor
until the pressure makes your head explode."

I write them back, begging that a chance be given
to my fella.
The girls have never taken to whales, they mate with
dolphins.
Males with perfectly proportioned bodies and pleasing
faces, wooing the crowd with their non-threatening
demeanor.

My whale takes me to dry land.

A romantic dinner complete with a water bucket
under the table.
After dinner, we walk towards the water.
He pushes my head down towards his cock.
It's too soon for the softness to fade though.
I need more time in his belly, more hand-holding
while the fire crackles.
My whale reacts harshly to my hesitation.

"I'm so sick of bitches playing games."

The end is coming.
I place detonation inside the fat layers
of his warm belly and swim back up to the surface.

Food Stamp Cuts

A plan to reduce the amount of food stamps
a needy family can receive has just went into
effect. A man that orders twelve dollar shots
of whiskey is thrilled to hear the news. He
wants to shout it from the mountaintops for
all to hear. He decides the bar is the soapbox.
He educates me on how it's hurting the poverty
stricken to provide them with assistance.

"Aid turns them into animals, incapable of feeding
themselves. They grow dependent on the help and
soon can't function without it. I'll take another
drink please."

I recall my years as an animal, living off government
assistance. The food stamp coupon book used to come
in the mail when I was little. I watched my Mama take
half of the vouchers and trade them in at apartment
37. The Hollamins ran a trade store out of their
apartment. You could exchange food stamp vouchers for
everything the grocery store said you couldn't.
Cigarettes, alcohol, porno mags, bags of skank weed,
and more importantly, makeup and hair products.
One pack of smokes that cost two dollars at the
gas station, cost you ten dollars in food stamp
vouchers.

Mama would trade over half of our food vouchers
(five kids in the house constantly hungry) for
smokes, wine, and makeup to smear on her face
to hide the damage the smokes and wine were doing.
I imagine going from Miss Teen Alabama to a busted
skank with five kids living in the projects, was
quite a challenge for her, but I felt no empathy
for my creator. I wanted strawberries. It's all I
thought about when we went grocery shopping.
Looking at the contents of our buggy was like

watching a puppy get ran over by a car. Potatoes,
beans, and cornmeal filled the metal grates.
I tried to hide a green basket filled with the
beautiful red berries inside once. Hoping the
cashier would get them rang up and bagged before
my Mama noticed. She caught them on the conveyor
belt, Slapped me across the face, and made me run
and put them back.

I hated being hit worse then I hated not eating
strawberries. I devised a plan in my mind to get
revenge in exactly thirty days.

Next month rolled around and I ran home to get the
mail before anyone else could. The envelope with
the vouchers was poking out of the top of the rusted
black mailbox. I opened it up, took a coupon book
for twenty dollars, and walked to the store by myself.

Two baskets for three dollars was the price of
my berries and I filled my cart.

"It's easier to ask for forgiveness, than permission."
some say.
I knew forgiveness was out of the question and I
didn't care. A sense of hopelessness spreads in
abusive homes and poverty stricken neighborhoods.
Growing numb to pain is actually one of the perks
to the situation.

I walked home and she was sitting on the porch smoking
a cigarette. I received a beating with my Daddy's
leather belt that afternoon.

She left purple bruises on my thighs and ass cheeks
for two weeks, but she did let me keep the
strawberries.

Harder Than a Preacher's Dick

Brother Tom knew God was love.
He drew tiny hearts on his underwear
and scribbled "Jesus Saves" just above
the skid marks on the back of his
whitey tighties.
Brother Tom sat in the front row of Sunday School.
His dick often got hard when Mrs. Donna
would begin to explain why Satan
was kicked out of Heaven.

He knew it was wrong and he felt shame.
He asked God to make his dick soft,
but his prayers went unanswered.

He folded up the worksheet that was handed out
and hid it in his back pocket. Once he got home,
he masturbated in the bathroom to the picture.
He ignored the burning flesh of the forsaken.
Brother Tom concentrated on the exposed breasts.
He imagined sucking the nipples, absorbing
the evil from the female body and saving her
from an eternity in hellfire.
He felt noble for this, but could feel Satan's hand
grow hot around his dick when he came.
He began paying penance by making roadside signs.
He placed withered plywood boards next to
highway exits with the message,
"Embrace Jesus" written in clumsy letters
with thick red paint.
Rain fell on the signs before they were dry,
and made the words bleed.

Southern Girl

There is no bond between us.
Me and the young girl on the beach in her rebel flag bikini.
She says heritage not hate, but doesn't know the name
of her swimsuit designer.
An old battle that gets carried for miles inside the worn straw basket
hanging off the side of a beaten down mule.

Mama tried to teach me the recipe as well.
Fear and ignorance stuffed inside a poverty stricken casserole
that all good Southern girls bring to the picnic.

The stars and bars highlight her tight firm ass as she
jumps in the water.
Antebellum sexpot.
Can she feel the pain of another woman?
Feel the Rebel pride of a slave girl shoved to the ground
in a cotton field.
The sharp thorn blossoms ripping her face as General Beauregard
rapes his property under the flag that waves above her head.
Rich white families of the South now sit in Cotton fields
posing for family pictures.
They smile for the camera, on land still moist with blood.

Delicate Man

Pretty lives lead to pretty words
that whisper out of pretty mouths.
Some can only dip their toe in
before an icy chill runs through
their bones.
Full submersion would pin their
lightweight endurance
to the bottom.
Drowning them with authentic imperfections.
They wait outside of delivery rooms.
They lock bathroom doors.
They demand that you stay hidden.

"But Mama, he quoted Milton."

"Naw Baby, he misquoted Milton.
You and I both know God is wicked.
That delicate man aint never gonna
put a chicken in the pot.
He turned his head when I went to
snapping it's neck."

Simple Woman

Trying to walk upright is difficult.
Her tornado mouth continuously forces me
backwards.
I could shake a bag of empty cans
and produce a more logical argument
than one of her confessions.

"It's my innards." she cries

The guts, eggs, and jiggly flesh that
she holds like a trophy over my head.
Peel a piece off
and the hormones spill out
like maggots.
Filling up your lungs
until you can't breathe in peace.

I'm a rat for staying.

For allowing nipples coated in honey butter
to soften the sound of her screech.

She plays a flute to lure me out of Town
and I follow the light between her thighs
into the smog.
Thick with wet tongues that make Vultures
flying overhead, blush with modesty.

I forget I'm a Man that understands the world.
I embrace the mud, the grime she smears on
me.
It leaves a stain long after she's gone.

The Lady Wants a Booth

Two men at the end of the bar
decide to call a taxi.

"Two shots of Jager to celebrate
this executive decision please." -they scream

Happy drunk people are a gift.
They wake me up when the monotony
of dispensing medicine to the sick
becomes too much.
But every now and then,
I get to see people at their best.

An elderly gentleman pushed the heavy
wooden door open, and held it
while the elderly woman rolled through
in her wheelchair.

I smiled at them and ran across the bar
to remove a chair from the table.
That's standard practice.
Remove the chair and adjust the table
so the wheelchair fits under.

"No thank you Ma'am. The Lady wants a booth.
She likes that corner one with the pretty
red light. It's more romantic."

He said it with the smile of a child
with a new toy.

"Yes, Sir. Whatever you need, you got it."

I stepped back and watched him.
He lifted her from the chair and placed her
on the bench. Scooting her small body slowly
down inside the booth.

Once she was snug and comfortable, she placed
her hand on top of his and patted it a few times.
She turned to me and asked for two martinis.

"Absolut straight up, extra dirty."

"Yes Ma'am. Right away."

I glanced over at them while I was washing
glasses, they were the only two people
in the room.

Afternoon Affair

Muddy boots squirm their way
down the trail to the water.
Within five minutes, she was
holding my hand.
Whistling while I remained silent
and enjoying the suction of our
finger's embrace.

I caught a fish.
Easy enough, but keeping them alive
has proven to be a problem.
We stopped on the way home
so she could have a drink,
or maybe five.
She told me of running in the sewers
as a child.
Dirty faced project kids with their
Daddy's flashlight.
Crawling their way through
shit lined tunnels.
Dodging rats and screaming
as loud as they could
in an effort to pierce their friend's eardrums
in the echoing cavern.

"Who was it that said that about the sewers
and looking up at the stars?"
She interrupts her own story to ask me.

"It was the gutter sweetie, not the sewers,
and it was Oscar Wilde."

"Well that's what I was doing way
back then in the sewers.
I was blinding the rats with my
flashlight and then kicking them."

I wanted her lips to fall off.
I knew it was a matter of time before she
opened her mouth and became that other person.
A barrage of backwoods abuse and poverty
soon followed that made me question whether
she was of sound mind and body.

I decided to write off her absurd words
to nerves and went forward with my plan
for a goodnight kiss.
Her dogs snarled and barked at me
through the front door while I leaned in
for our first kiss.
The moment foreshadowed a chaos that I knew
she would bring into my life if I kept ignoring
the signs that told me to run, but the madness
felt good.
It felt better than all the empty days and nights
that she wasn't sharing her absurd words with me.

James DJ's at the Strip Club

His dick is a combine harvester
clocking in overtime in a field
of sticky wheat.
He wants more than this marathon
of pussy plowing, but fails at bonding
every time.
His dick goes numb with every encounter.
Frustrated and afraid, he pretends.
He needs her to stay, so he eats her pussy
and wears a mask.
He waits for her to fall asleep before he
masturbates in the closet.
This arrangement can only keep a woman
for so long.
Eventually their ego will get tied into his inability
to climax inside them.
They will find fault in themselves
and start to feel undesirable in his eyes.
They all leave him.
No amount of honesty on James's part, can
coax them into staying.

I tell him to slow down
and clean out his system.
Maybe the effects of being
overstimulated have broken
the natural order of things.

"Get a new job, go for a walk
in the woods, and no sex or
internet porn for a month."

He laughs at my advice and looks
at his phone. A picture of a pair
of tits covered in semen is calling.
He picks it up.

Steve Buys a Sex Doll

"How do you fellas get the heater coil to stop buzzing around in her sugarbox? Can I order a spare part from the factory or just change a fuse?"

Steve gave up after Susan left him.
Two years of isolation began crushing him inside.
He avoided colleagues at lunch so their stories
couldn't hurt him
Jokes and musings about their wives and girlfriends and
all the warm moments and smiles that no woman
would ever share with him.
The heart knows what it wants, but it needs a hitman.
The brain can do the dirty work so the heart stays clean.
Adapt your perception of reality and fill the need.

"The blond with the sweet dimples, I think she's lovely."

"Oh, yeah, that's Molly. She's got silicone injected vagina lips
and a five year warranty. If she gets any mold or rippage in her
anal, we'll replace the entire asshole for free."

Steve wished the clerk wasn't so vulgar about Molly's
private parts. Her asshole was no longer his business.
She was with Steve now, and he would take care of her.
Steve held Molly tight as he carried her to his car.
He told the story of his first homerun in little league
on the way home.

Shady

The company
he keeps,
reeks.

Swollen pigs
exposing flabby
flesh.
Shaking
hot pink guts
at the boys
walking home
from school.
Some men lay
with swine.
They black out
their eyes
before diving in
the mud.

The stains show through
white dinner jackets
that ladies require of
Gentleman callers.
The Pig-Fuckers will
try to win their hand
with a slaughter.

Beating the swine in
the Town Square for
squealing about.
The poor sows refuse
to defy their man.
They swallow humiliation
like so much cum and gruel.
Accepting the cruelty from
a hand that once wallowed
in the filth.

The ladies in the audience
can feel the Pig's beating.
They ask him to show mercy
and accept his past.

He honors
their request
in the hopes
that his
red transgression
can become
soft yellow hues.
His appetite will never
be satisfied by virtue.
It can't be sullied by
stained fingertips.
He will instead
wear out the trail
in the woods
that leads to
the hog pen.
They'll always be waiting,
fat guts exposed.

Chuck E. Cheese

The man in the giant rat costume
is giving it all he's got.
He must have a background in dance.
The kids swarm him.
Their sticky fingers getting caught up
in his fur, weighing down the performance.
He feels the chains of his tiny audience
wrapped tight around his throat.

Surrounded by youth, he sees the days pass.
Children sucking the time away from adults
in a greedy vortex of needs.

Do not let their voracity for time
make you bitter.
They are no more to blame than the sun is,
for rising up and stealing the moonlight's glow.

Just dance, dance like the giant rat
those kids need you to be.
You can stare at the Mom's tight asses
in yoga pants on your break.

Stink

He tries harder than most men.
I take notice of his effort.
He swears that we will be
peas and carrots, one day.
He is wrong.
My suitor lacks the stomach
to be my carrot.
We could go for a swim,
but I would hold his head under
until he stopped kicking.
His sensitive nature would sink
in a pool of blood and bones.
Best we sit side by side as friends.
Friends who welcome each other's
thoughts and ideas, with no plans
to imprison them.

Sugar Ray

Vance is serious about his art.
His mixed martial art that requires skill, dedication,
and what looks like steroids falling out of a bottle
onto the bar.

He has small eyes and a confused face.
Constantly looking for ways to settle the score
with less masculine men.
Men who may have tormented or abused him
before he discovered creatine powder and
sleeveless shirts.

Vance tells me what it takes to be a true warrior in the cage.
He can wrestle his opponent to the ground, or out move them
with his boxing prowess.
I tell him about my boy being a natural born boxer.
How I used to call him Sugar Ray when he would breastfeed.

"The greedy runt would get a mouthful of boobie and start punching
the hell out of my breasts trying to get more milk to come out."

Vance grinned just enough to be polite and started back with his
how to be a warrior speech.
I excused myself and hid behind the mug cooler to read.
Peeking out from behind every five minutes,
until the coast was clear.

The Moon is Following

He changes shape
depending on my daily chores.

A freight train barrelling through
a field of raspberries, he fills his basket
while I sit in traffic.

He's a giant Magnolia, puckering up
to the sun.
Allowing the wind to blow his scent
across my front porch.
It hangs in the air as I swing back
and forth.

A thief breaking in my window.
His pale light lays next to me on my bed,
tucked in a corner, like a gentleman waiting
to dream.

Good Mother

One theory suggests serial killers
start out with animals.
Dahmer killed critters in the woods
and stuck their heads atop wooden
poles and placed them in a circle.
He had a ceremony of sorts.
Are the Mamas of these budding villains
without blame?

Imagine the Queen in Aliens,
her big slick belly and
beautiful strength.
The understanding of when a skull
needs to be cracked, even when
that skull once grew inside of you,
the creator.

I was told of a young man who buried a cat
in the front yard, and ran it over with a lawn
mower.

"His parents were going through a divorce,
I'm sure it will be ok, he just needs someone
to talk to."

- Shirley Franks
PTA Vice President Little River Elementary

Is it ok?
Does he need someone to talk to,
or is he broke beyond repair?

Screams from the stands at my son's little league
ballgame sound like orders on a battlefield.

Keeping my boy in the shit, will make him tough.

"I'm sick of all this pussy ass shit where everyone
gets a trophy. These kids need to feel loss and regret.
They need to try harder to prove to their parents that
they love them enough to win. Sort out the winners
from the losers already."

- Scotty Laroy,
t-ball coach 5yr old pee-wee league

Breeding hate is easy I say,
love hides it's imperfections
and Mama's cuddle their future
villains blindly.

Road Crew

Would you throw that
stop sign to the ground
and run away with me?
I'm afraid you would find
nothing but disappointment
if you left the road crew.
There is no escape inside
my car.
I would have found it by now.
I can take you to the lake if you'd like.
I'll listen all night while you scream about
burned macaroni in the bottom of your mama's pan
and every opportunity your father threw away
to give you a decent example of how a man should act.
You'll feel better in the morning when you notice
the fog hanging on top of the water.
The lake has digested your words and started to breath.

We Got a Break in the Cold

Forty degrees may not bother some
people. It cripples me and my greedy
love of the heat. Sticky moisture and
blaring sun is a perfect day.

I walked outside to sit in the grass
and my son showed up with his sketchpad.
He asked if I was writing and I told him
yes. He then asked if he could sit outside
to do his origami.

"It feels different when I work outside on
my stuff." he says

"I know it does. It's nice huh?"

"Yeah, it's cool."

He didn't sit beside me. He walked over
to the patio table and started drawing.
I feel close to him in these times.
Watching someone you love, do something
you love, is such a nice gift.

Dimebags

He was thirty four and slept inside
a hollowed out pine tree.
Climbing inside every night
his bare skin
absorbed the moonlight
that shined through
the open nooks.

A handsome young man
who longed to leave the forest
and cultivate a life inside
a box structure.

He dreamed of walking into Town
stealing an axe
and coming back
to chop down the Pine tree
that provided contentment.

Rage was missing.
Fear was missing.

His hand no longer carved
the struggles of emotion
and pain.
It ran smooth lines
down the backside of a Sycamore.

Quiet acceptance formed an umbrella
over the lovers that lay under its canopy.
He needed to burn it's limbs to the ground.

Lacking the strength to simply stay away
and allow another to slumber inside her nooks.
He would destroy her before allowing another
to feel the warm pulp.

Sister

The cornfield is lush and the wind carries
sugar in the air. Two sisters go hiding in
the stalks. Ripping open the ears to pull
out the silk and collect a basket full.
The scarecrow hangs over them, like Jesus
in his starring role. The older sister
digs into the ground when the crow flies over.
She cups the dirt with little hands and piles
it on the side. Going deeper every time until
the cold earth calms her. She plants her head
face down in the soil and waits. The younger
sister watches the crow fly. Her black wings
sparkle blue pearl against the sun. She perches
herself on the scarecrow's shoulder and begins
to peck a hole in his chest. The burlap sack
unraveling little by little as the crow empties
him out. She winks at the little sister and caws
"Let's see if you can fix that." before flying off.

First Date

His annoyance is no match
for my polka dot dress.
I'm going to float away from the table
and imagine his hands on my face.
If only my coos were a bit more
dove-like, and less circling vulture.
Restraint is mastered by women with
clogged veins and sleepy eyes.
Should our discussion be anything less
than natural and organic?
Trying to smile and entertain a serious
man is draining the pool and cracking
skulls the minute someone decides to do
a backflip.
We could live together in a library and pretend
all the books are filled with lies.

Do Something With Your Hair

I was so foreign to you.
Your very own seedling, sprouting
disappointment out of your vagina.
Mama laid in bed wearing her pageant crown
and lifted her skirt to expose me to the world.
She reached inside her pussy
hoping to find a fleshy little sack
of diamonds, but chipped her nails
on a bag of rocks.
She threw me to the ground and recoiled
in horror at the lack of brilliance.
Women are born cultivators.
They can manipulate the soil to produce
a harvest, big enough to fill their own
needs.
Mama began to apply ancient techniques.
Passed down traditions she learned from
her Mama of how to break down self-image.

Little girls that can't at least try
to be pretty, don't deserve to eat.
Pin their hands down on a hot stove.
The burned skin tissue will remind them
to brush their hair when company is coming over.

Chokehold

Contours of soft forgiving flesh
spilled over
into the hard creases of his face.

His head nuzzled and rooted
until perfectly cradled
between tender flushed skin.

The warmth of her bosom
absorbed every drop of failure
that exploded from a broken man.

He woke with the sun and scampered away
trying to pretend he was still a man.

Dark Pig

I know your bite.
We share the same eggs
hidden deep in our belly.
You once struck my hand
with a wooden spoon.
Reaching for the bowl of
grits without thanking
Jesus first, earned me that.

We are in another lifetime now.
Words fall out like manic bird
chirpings.
Our memories have the same shape
but yours are blue and mine are gray.
These people, these parents that
we broke ourselves against are
strangers to me when you speak.
I envy your cunning.
You stalk the dark pig and wait
for him to root up from the mud.
He breathes with flared nostrils
and you hack off his head.

I stalk him in the night, but lack
the strength to send him away.

Nightgown

A sudden gust of stank
confronts me as I peruse
the paperbacks at Goodwill.

Three shelves of used books
go unnoticed by the blue hairs
searching for another pantsuit.

One by one they snatch and push
another elastic waist nightmare
down a crowded rack of cotton blends.

I notice a familiar piece of fabric
get sent further down the pole
at the veiny hands of a grandma
in a Tazmanian Devil sweatshirt.

Could it be?
It looks identical to mama's old nightgown.
Paper thin ruffles on the collar
embroidered roses along the sleeves
and a smoke stained glow
emitting like a supernova
over a park full of doublewides.

The magic hit me like a teenaged mom
with a fresh G.E.D. in her glovebox
and I decided to try it on.

The frail nightie clung to my body
like it had been waiting for me
to resurrect it's powers.

The sudden urge to chain-smoke Kent Golden Lights
and scream "Get the fuck off my porch ya heatherns."
while slapping some kid upside the head
with my dirty flattened out house slipper

made my blood run cold.

I soon came to my senses
and knew what had to be done.

The nightgown must be destroyed.

I must purchase the cursed cloth
douse it in gasoline
and cremate her
inside the blazing inferno
of my fire pit -
being careful not to alert the neighbors
to my plan.

Hangnail

I lose words
when I open my mouth.
My tongue goes limp in fear,
only nervous
ticks,
tick,
tick.
Try to curl
and form a response,
only to produce an erratic
bastard language.

If your face was a pillow,
I could carve out a spot
and live happily.

You would suffocate from my greed.

I would pull a goose feather
from your lips once you succumbed.
Wear it proudly in my hair after you departed.

Sold

Moments can be taken away.
The height of everything we are
is in the sharing of words, not
the touch of flesh, and yet the
craving of a calloused hand can
trick the self into destruction.

My first poem was sold and it's
covered in a blanket of intended
smut. My Mama is laughing like a
jackass at being right about me.
She's holding my head down and
threatening to burn my eye sockets
out with the cherry from her cigarette
unless I confess what she already knows.

"I am born to a coven of witches that
rise only through filth."

I am no better than her in thought.
Only through action can I pretend to
not have climbed through a rotten womb
on my way to the light.

Oliver

When things get messy
the mind has to assume command.
Fear of losing the taste,
the authentic feel of penetration.
Mouths to feed, mouths to feed, is
the mantra that gets repeated when
loneliness suffocates.
Running out of dog food is a forgivable
offense, permitting you have an equally
appetizing alternative.
Leftover pineapple pizza gets sliced up
and placed in their food dish.
Hank is simple and brings me comfort.
He is a gobbler and wastes no time
in chomping up his breakfast.
Oliver is the beautiful one.
His blond fur dances with sunbeams
when he gives chase.

He sniffs the pizza and gives me his
"Eat shit and die" look, and walks away
without a single bite.

"I'm doing the best I can!" I scream at
him as he walks down the stairs on the
back porch.
"You act like you didn't have worms hanging
out of your ass and covered in filth and
fleas when I found you. I don't remember
any Pedigree Dog Shows trying to get in
touch with you to perform in their shows.
I'm all you got, you judgmental fucking
prick. Quit making me feel like shit."

Oliver doesn't stick around for the rest
of my breakdown. He lays beneath the Dogwood
tree and licks his paws. He looks up at me
on the porch for a moment and I flick him
off with my middle finger.

Rowing

Night after night I dream you alive.
Your throat shaking from the cold.
Hair slick-backed and wet from the
dew.
I'll play possum if you attempt to
pull back the covers.
Break your spine and turn your bones
into paper.
My little paper man will be placed inside
a little paper boat.
Stay inside and row down the river where
you belong.
Don't stop to pick flowers for me.
Keep rowing till you get home.

Turkeys Hate Janet Jackson

He stared at me inside my car
and refused to move.
Maybe Thanksgiving or maybe the current
situation in the middle east,
but something has gotten Bob's turkey
all kinds of pissed up.
He chases my tires and struts his
neck back and forth.

"Hey, fuck you bitch, watch my dance
why don't cha?"

I oblige him, and turn up the radio.
Janet starts blaring out the window-

"Oh you nasty boy."

Turkey freaks out and starts jumping on top
of my hood. I'm forced to scream at Bob-

"Bob, come get your turkey, goddammit, before
he fucks up my paint."

Bob came out and scooted Turkey back in
the fence.
I felt bad for Turkey as I watched
him scuttle away.
He knows the world is a shit box.

About the Author

Misty Cosgrove has a long history of being successful at life. She's taken home the first place ribbon at the Georgia State Fair Chili Cook Off, TWICE, and is currently the reigning Champion of the Women's Southeast Division Mud Wrestling Association. This is her first book of poetry.

NeoPoiesis: *a new way of making*

1) in ancient Greece, poiesis referred to the process of making: creation - production - organization - formation - causation

2) a process that can be physical and spiritual, biological and intellectual, artistic and technological, material and teleological, efficient and formal

3) a means of modifying the environment and a method of organizing the self, the making of art and music and poetry, the fashioning of memory and history and philosophy, the construction of perception and expression and reality

4) an independent publisher with a steadfast goal to print and promote outstanding poets, writers and artists that reflect the creative drive and spirit of the new electronic landscape

NeoPoiesisPress.com

www.ingramcontent.com/pod-product-compliance
Lightning Source LLC
LaVergne TN
LVHW091229080426
835509LV00009B/1220